# THE ULTIMATE DAD'S SURVIVAL GUIDE

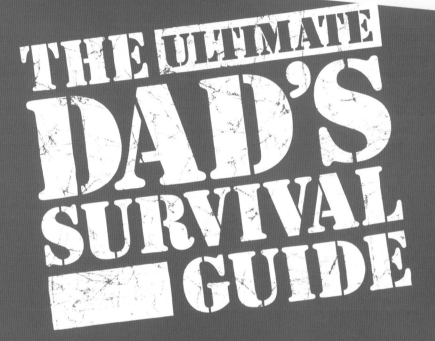

## Written by Dr. Ian Banks

and Killian Kavanagh

# Dear Fellow Dads,

Balancing your home and working lives can be a difficult challenge but my golden rule is "if Moma ain't happy, nobody happy" and it's a good starting point.

Speaking as a man who is always in the poo, just varying depths, I put together some basic suggestions for a utopian home and family life which I got writer Doctor Ian Banks to put it in words. From my own experience there are ways we dads can work smarter rather than harder and still have a bit of time to ourselves.

Whether your partner is a list writer, clean freak, logistic psycho organiser or blissfully cruezie, likes football and tells you to go to the pub and enjoy yourself regularly, hopefully there is something in this little book for you.

On the children front there is no one right way to raise your kids. I have watched a lot of my peers embark on fatherhood with a calm controlled exterior, but through their eyes you can see the fear. After all, eyes are the windows to the soul.

Sure you're delighted when you hear the news, but then the reality sets in – anxiety at the prospect of having children, the fear of the unknown and the prospect of massive changes to your lifestyle. Then there's the birth, the early years with sleep deprivation – and let's not forget that first nappy change. Ah yes, the first nappy. I remember it well. It's up there with remembering where you were when you heard Elvis or Lady Diana had died.

A cruel fact of life is that kids grow up fast and before you know it they will be asking for the keys to your car. So take the time to enjoy your kids, before they become teenagers and don't want to know you.

And don't forget to keep your relationship thriving, as eventually it will be just the two of you again.

Anyway, that's enough from me. Let's get you prepared for what lies ahead. Good luck!

## Killian Kavanagh

# GEMS OF WISDOM INSIDE THIS BOOK

Concept **Killian Kavanagh** killian@four5one.ie

Words **Ian Banks.** Illustrations **Terry Willers.** Editorial Consultant **Lucy Taylor.** Printed by **Total Print.**
The Dad's Survival Guide is published and designed by **FOUR5ONE CREATIVE** www.four5one.com

# GETTING OUT OF TROUBLE

Caring for kids can sometimes feel like juggling a number of rapidly moving balls and averting disasters at every turn. Fill in these pages to give yourself a handy reference of important contact numbers and dates.

## Important contact numbers

**Wife/Partner's Mobile**

**Grandparents' Number**

**Doctor's Name & Number**

**Dentist's Name & Number**

**Teacher's Name & Number**

**Childminder/Creche Name & Number**

**Babysitter's Name & Number**

# Important dates & other information

**School holidays**

**School in-service days**

**Birthdays**

Name                                    Date

**Wedding anniversary**

**Mother's Day**

**Mother In Law's Birthday**

**VHI Membership Number**

**Ideal Human Temperature**

**Other Useful Information**

# EXPECTING

## Reacting to the news of pregnancy

Not all men are ecstatic on hearing the good news and there are invariably mixed emotions. Tearing all your hair out and ripping up your season ticket to Manchester United will not go down well.

A bottle of champagne (of which you will be able to drink almost all quite legitimately) will however in all senses of the word, go down well.

You are going to have an interesting nine months with a finale that throws the Cup Final into a cocked hat, but mood swings are inevitable as the hormones kick in.

Fads are common (stock up on carrots, coal, very expensive Belgian chocolates, etc). You may also find your partner has mood swings as well.

**Mood swings are inevitable as the hormones kick in**

## Early days, happy returns

Morning sickness baffles most men. Chundering after 10 pints and a curry is perfectly reasonable behaviour but to wake up with pursed lips and wide expectant eyes is patently odd. This can be so bad, especially in the first two semesters (6 months) women sometimes dehydrate, lose weight and need to be admitted to hospital.

There is probably nothing you can do when it gets this bad but for the less traumatic versions many women find tricks to reduce the sickness. A small dry biscuit with a cup of tea or milk is a common strategy but it only works if it is there when she first awakes.

**Five minutes too late and your pillow has a permanent Stilton flavour.**

## Two to Tango

When it comes to making babies Aristotle had a theory. The woman provided the canvas while the man supplied the paint. Supplying the canvas can be pretty hard work, not least because your weight is steadily increasing, pressure is building up on your diaphragm, bladder and digestive system and most importantly, your hormones are doing a Samba with your emotions. Being heavier is not just the problem, it's being heavier just in one place, the front. This puts strain on the back muscles, so bending over or simply standing up straight becomes increasingly difficult. Watching out for when she has something to pick up and darting in like Sir Walter Raleigh, the bicycle fanatic, or giving a back massage during the day as well as at night and more to the point, doing the housework all make for better Tangos, if not Sambas.

## Natural but nasty

Be prepared for fire in the hole. Heartburn is common during pregnancy, not least because of the pressure on the stomach. Your kind offer to cook all the meals will be less gratefully received if vindaloo, Chilli Con Carne and deep fried Mars Bars are the only things on the menu. Smaller, frequent, more easily digested meals on the other hand will be deeply and more permanently appreciated. A nocturnal glass of ice cold milk on hand makes for similar affection. Your stainless steel fishing vacuum flask has never found a more productive use.

# Antenatal classes

Women in their first pregnancy where there is some reason to want closer observation or if a previous pregnancy was a bit hairy, are often advised full hospital care. Parental classes are usually held in the hospital antenatal department and you are welcome to come along to these sessions, especially for the first ultrasound scan. Never underestimate how scared your partner can be at that first session. A hot sweaty hand in her hotter sweatier hand helps more than you will know.

A hot sweaty hand in her hotter sweatier hand can really help

It's easy to forget in that darkened room with the glowing totally incomprehensible screen that abnormalities are rare and all unusual positions in the womb can be safely dealt with. Now is not the time to mention that you get a better picture on Channel 5. Or maybe it is just exactly the right time.

# Great training

Getting up in the middle of the night is par for the course when having kids. So your partner's frequent excursion to the loo (pressure on the bladder), constant shifting in the bed (due to pressure) and irrational demands for a life saving Belgian chocolate at 3am (hormone shifts) should be seen as great training. Leave the light on in the loo, buy a better mattress, give great massage and work out the shortest route to the all night delicatessen. It will toughen you up boy, for the big push to come later.

Sudden, swift and severe shifts in mood are also part of the equation as her hormones leap around like demented jugglers. Expect weeping followed by ecstatic laughter at banal baby-product adverts. Join in. It has to be better than a party political broadcast.

Now is the time for being Nelson Mandela not George Bush. Just because she can't explain why the bedroom has to be painted pink, the baby cot erected from a flat pack, the stairs cordoned off like East Berlin at 1am six months before the baby is even due doesn't mean it's not perfectly reasonable to her.

**Her hormones will leap around like demented jugglers with weeping followed by ecstatic laughter**

# Labour

If you feel a tad apprehensive about childbirth try to see it from your partner's point of view. Imagine pulling your top lip over your head while passing a rugby ball out of your bum. Now add some malicious bastard shouting 'push' right in your ear, while a guy in a white coat with arms like a gorilla keeps checking to see if the ball needs a touch more air.

In truth, watching someone you love in pain is not easy to deal with and most men would gladly swap places. Well, after a couple of stiff whiskeys anyway. This is not helped by a wide eyed horizontal stare. "This is all your fault you vindictive swine. You did this to me."

Most important to remember and get through to your partner is that it will end. Most pain is endurable so long as there is an end to it. This is made easier by having someone there whom they trust to tell them there is an incredible thing happening which is far better to focus on than the pain.

Whatever pain relief path she chooses, you can supply a cool towel on the forehead, back rubbing and most of all, encouragement.

Remember, pain is relative. Your crushed fingers will soon regain their circulation and feeling

Some people say men don't belong at the delivery. It's up to you two, not the midwife or doctor. It's your baby.

# WHO'S

LETS FACE IT, HEALTH PROFESSIONALS ALL LOOK ALIKE, DON'T BE AFRAID TO ASK WHO THEY ARE AND WHAT THEY DO

# WHO?

# Health Visitors

Nurses with extra training for caring in the community. Generally they will visit about 10 days after the baby is born and check whether you or your partner have any problems, need any help or whether you are both still breathing.

# General Practitioners

GPs are less involved in delivery but can be more responsible for ante-natal care. Few are prepared to deliver at home but may do so in community hospitals. The lounge suit is a dead giveaway.

# Obstetricians

These are doctors specialising in pregnancy, labour and often gynaecology. Most women will see the consultant infrequently during antenatal care unless there is a particular reason for doing so. Most complicated deliveries are performed by obstetricians. If you or your partner are concerned you can ask to see them during your antenatal visit or book in for the next one.

# Paediatricians

These doctors are generally on hand during a complicated birth or a caesarean section. They will check the baby shortly after birth to make sure all is well and are the person to talk through any concerns over the baby. They can build towers with six blocks and will turn their heads to the sound of a ball in a cup.

# Midwives

Predominately, but not exclusively female, they will deliver most babies and perform most ante natal checks. They can work exclusively in either hospital or the community or sometimes work in both environments. Biting the heads off snakes is no longer part of midwife training.

# AND THEN COMES BABY...

## Choosing baby's name

Names need to end in an 'a', 'o' or 'n' to shout later in life when finding your favourite CD melted into an ash tray. You can't make the 'p' of Philip last nearly as long or sonically devastating as the 'n' in Killian. Mothers can turn the 'a' in Angela into a half decent cruise missile.

Resist the temptation to name your first son after a top football player. Most of them will be playing for Tranmere Rovers by the time he realises who he is.

Only name them after yourself with great care. Girls called Sidney often find it difficult to strike up a meaningful relationship in later life.

**The name you give your child could have a devastating effect on their later years**

# SEX BEFORE AND AFTER BABY

## Sex during pregnancy

Strict rules used to be enforced over sex during pregnancy, but as the baby is virtually immune from harm during love making, sex is safe at all stages of pregnancy, right up to the date the baby is due. A too liberal interpretation of this general observation can provide no end of entertainment for the labour ward staff.

**THERE ARE SOME IMPORTANT EXCEPTIONS REQUIRING CAUTION AND ADVICE AND POSSIBLY ABSTINENCE FROM PENETRATIVE SEX.**

**IF THERE HAVE BEEN:**
- Repeated miscarriages
- A series of premature labours
- Placenta praevia
  (where the placenta lies close to or over the opening of the womb)
- If there is any bleeding during intercourse
- If the waters have already broken

## Sexual desire

Male attitudes vary towards the appearance of their partner as pregnancy changes her shape. Some men find it very attractive, while others confess, often guiltily, that they find it a big turn-off. Spending a longer time in body contact with each other, without being demanding will help maintain confidence in your relationship.

# Sex after baby

There is no biological reason why you cannot resume intercourse as soon as both of you wish to do so after the baby is born. As with sex during pregnancy, there can be ways of making sex more enjoyable or even possible after the baby is born.

Many doctors advise a six week break after delivery, but it is up to you and your partner so long as common sense prevails. Once the stitches are out – either from an episiotomy or caesarean section – it is a matter of comfort as there is little danger from infection or harm from gentle love-making. Even so, your partner will probably respond more to caring, empathic consideration.

Different positions such as a cushion under her hips or lying side by side may help.

Lubricating gels can overcome dryness of the vagina which may follow from the change in hormones.

# Changing libido

Libido you both enjoyed before the baby may not be the same afterwards but like swings and roundabouts, there are gains and losses. In the main, the losses are temporary while the gains are permanent.

# Myths about sex and your baby

**Penetrative, vaginal sex causes an abortion.**
**Untrue.** The penis cannot enter the womb. Your doctor will advise you if there are any good medical reasons not to do so.

**Sex can damage the baby.**
**Untrue.** The baby is well out of harm's way during intercourse. It is possible to introduce sexually transmitted diseases such as HIV which could affect your partner and possibly your baby but you can be tested for these complaints. Meanwhile, use condoms, male or female.

**Sex can lead to premature labour.**
**Untrue.** There is no evidence for this although there are some conditions in which caution should be exercised.

**An orgasm when pregnant will injure the baby or start labour prematurely.**
**Untrue.** An orgasm can bring on contractions which are normally present towards the end of pregnancy called "Braxton Hicks" contractions. They will settle on their own in a short time. Previous premature labours may require caution and your doctor will advise you.

# HAPPY NAPPY VS DANGEROUS DIAPER

Brace yourself: Nappies are going to change their appearance as baby gets older but your fingernails are never going to smell the same again. Check this out by scratching the small box next to each nappy description.

## Version #1

Immediately after birth they will probably pass a green/black goo called meconium and is simply all the debris built up in the bowels during development in the womb.

## Mellow Yellow

As milk is increasingly digested you will see a yellow/orange colour. Breast fed babies tend to have less solid motions than bottle fed. They also smell 'sweeter'. Like adults there is no 'normal' number of motions.

## Wot, no poo Nappy?

None for more than a few days or profuse watery motions needs a doctors attention.

## Mother of all nappies

Stools can be so large you wonder how on earth they fitted in such a tiny body. Unfortunately they can cause small tears at the anus which makes passing subsequent motion very painful. Bright red blood streaked on the outside of the stool is common in these cases but any blood in the motion must be reported to your doctor.

Now get out the nail brush.

## Always change a baby on the floor.
Never a table or bar stool.

## Disposable nappies are actually reusable. To a point.

## Keep your fingers dry and free from anything greasy.
The reusable tabs will not work otherwise. Worse still they come apart under pressure if you catch the drift. Believe me, you will.

## Boy babies should have the pointy bit downwards.
Otherwise you will be changing nappies every half hour.

# TOP TIPS

## There is always the option of not changing a nappy.
You may get away with it once but never twice. A red, sore rash forms around their wee bum caused by the ammonia in their wee. If you are still unconvinced squirt some oven cleaner down your Y fronts.

## The ultimate answer is to get someone else to change the nappy.
I once changed a nappy in a supermarket surrounded by women. They couldn't stand it and immediately dived in to help. One woman stood back smiling. "Well done", she said. "I get flat tyres changed by men the same way"."

# FEEDING

## Babies do not eat. They feed. This is important.

We eat when we are often not hungry. Babies don't. So avoid strict regimes of time either forcing baby to eat or cry right up until the next feed 'is due'.

## Texture is just as important as flavour to a baby.

As they get older they appreciate coarser food.

## Experiment with foods.

What they point blank refuse one day they gobble up the next. Like the train whooshing into the tunnel a the end of Hitchcock's North by North West, subtlety can often be more effective than crude effort. Going Choo, Choo while waving the spoon full of food around before disappearing into the tunnel works better than force feeding. Babies wouldn't know a train if it bit them on their bare bum so they are probably humouring us sad dads.

## Don't ever wear your best gear when feeding.

Put a few sheets of newspaper under the seat and keep kitchen roll close at hand.

## For night feeding divide the work load.

One sleeps the other feeds. You can sleep at work like all new fathers do.

# Breast-feeding is best for everyone.

Although there is conflicting advice about babies sleeping in the same bed as mum and dad. Best available advice is not to feed in bed. If bottle feeding get everything sorted before bedtime.

**Don't preheat milk and leave for longer than 20 minutes for risk of gastroenteritis.**

**Teat hole too small =** frustrated baby = crying baby = dad eating own elbow.

**Teat hole too big =** wet baby = damp sheets on dad's side of the bed.

**Keep teat full of milk.** If air gets into baby it has to get back out and it usually brings most of everything else with it.

**If air gets into baby it has to get back out**

# TEETHING

Front teeth appear at around 6 months.

Molars appear at around one year.

After 18 months
the canines
come through

Chewing fingers, hot cheeks and irritability
accompany particularly the front and molars.

Put coolable teething rings in the fridge
(not freezer) for maximum relief.
They work well for baby as well.

# SHOPPING WITH BABY

Choose your shop carefully.

Look for good parking without tank trap bollards.

Find a good solid trolley with a proper baby seat

**Look for changing facilities for dads as well**

Hanging around women's toilets is just sad, dad.

## Look for wide aisles

Go to shops with no sweets at child eye-level.

**Give them a paper bag which rustles seductively to play with not a toy.** You will be bending over continuously picking up toys and end up like Uriah Heap.

# TRANSPORT

Accidents involving children in cars are unfortunately common. Distraction from children fighting/crying/climbing out of the sun-roof is a common cause. Keep cool. Pull over if you want to shout and wave your hands around.

Comfy, well restrained seats and belts make the journey easier for all.

Remember: It is a legal requirement for children to belt up in the back.

Take a favourite toy on a long journey with baby

**Are they bored?**
Bring toys/books/games etc.

**Are they tired?**
Bring a blanket and cushions. Suggest they snuggle down for a while (but still in their seatbelts).

**Are they hungry/thirsty?**
Bring bread and tasty snacks rather than just sweets which make them feel more hungry later.

**Are they restless?**
Pull off into a café or picnic area. It will not get any better, so sooner is better than later.

**Are they aliens who have taken over your normally wonderful children's bodies?**
Relax, in an Espace no one can hear you scream.

# Car baby seats

## The seat must be the correct size for your child.

Ask shop assistants for advice rather than guessing. Take the child with you, saves buying a tape measure. Most shops will advise you. The seat must surround the child's head.

## Ensure correct fitting into your car and any other car you are likely to use it in.

It's worth asking the retailer to demonstrate how the seat fits and check it is suitable for your vehicle. Securing clamps must stay in place if the seat is to stay safe. Get advice from a qualified mechanic if necessary.

## The shoulder harness must allow for growth by maintaining a correct fit over the shoulders.

Make sure you go for padded harnesses to prevent chest damage on impact.

## Unless impossible to fit, you should always favour rearward facing seats.

These generally offer better protection than forward-facing models particularly in front impact accidents. Obviously this only works while they fit into a baby seat. Afterwards use the correct seat belts for their size.

## Air-bag protection systems can harm a child by hitting their head but not supporting their body.

Always read the car manufacturer's information. You may need to disable the system, particularly in the front passenger seat. Effective seat belts are then even more vital. This depends on the size of the child rather than simply age. Ask your car dealer for advice.

Ask for a cuddle and you're just as likely to get a Liverpool kiss from a toddler

# TODDLER

Babies are born without knee caps.
They don't appear until they are 2-6 years old.
This is why they only use their heads as part of
a Liverpool kiss. An eye-to-eye quick cuddle
and squeeze can mean a trip to the dentist.

'Home alone' does happen. A quick scan for
anything breathing at knee height keeps you out
of the newspapers.

An unbreakable toy is useful for breaking other toys.

## The box in which a toy arrived is often more attractive than the toy itself.

Play hide and seek, caravans and Jack-in-the-box on demand. Hell, you paid for the wrapping as well as the state-of-the-art robotic dog.

## A tyre hung by rope from a tree provides more fun than a construction set for older kids...

and gives some insight into breaking strains not to mention Dad's weight.

## The best way to make sure a weed is a weed and not a valuable plant is for your toddler to pull on it.

If it comes out of the ground easily, it is a valuable plant.

## Never, ever put weedkiller into lemonade bottles.

Keep it in the original packaging and out of reach.

### Children love to chase mowers

Every year children lose their feet as they slide under the cutter.
Keep them off mowers and out of the garden when mowing.

### Organic weeding = children's fun

Slave labour by any other name, but hey, watch those daises disappear.

# NEGOTIATING MINEFIELDS

Having an animal to lavish affection on also teaches responsibility towards dependant creatures. Unless they adopt an elephant or sperm whale they will out-live them. While often emotionally devastating it does serve to introduce mortality into their thoughts. Giving a reason can make the difference and some dads will replace the departed poisson with another. Fine, so long as it is not a finger feeding trained piranha.

## Hamster

Merely imitating most politicians, the hamster may be dead but the wheel is still turning.

## Goldfish

Simply doing the back stroke. You once could have replaced this fish by simply tearing the clothes off its child owner and stopping a rag and bone man. Sadly, they are all now in the scrap yard in the sky. Or being eaten by vengeful goldfish in hell.

## Cat

Felines have nine lives. It must have really enjoyed itself through the previous eight. Make no mention of Davy Crocket or 'not enough room to'.

## Dog

Dyslexic canine atheists still wonder about the existence of dog. Sad as it is, children do accept a replacement for a dead dog which is only two letters short of dad.

# Reasoning with children

## First, get something clear.
## You are not the master in your own house.
If your child asks you can he do "something" and you say, "sounds reasonable" don't be surprised if your partner comes into your sanctuary with, "Why did you let him out when I grounded him?". Next time insist on a signed letter from their mother, preferably supported by bar-coded authorisation. Not that this will reduce your status when they return from a mothers restricted zone. "Just wait until your father gets home. He will use Semtex for your ear-plugs".

**As Chairman Mao nearly said,**
**"Speak with a loud voice and carry a very small stick".**

## Hostage negotiation
### Getting one child to give the other child their toy back
Politicians are well aware that there are only two ways to get people to change their ways and relieve their grasp on tax:
- **Threaten terrible punishment**
- **Offer something in return**

Children are not actually people but the same thing applies. Opening the doors to Hell for a child who has taken her brother's favourite toy only works once. The second time round she remembers the Earth failing to open up beneath her. Bribery, while not always ethical in politics certainly helps with a childhood hostage situation. But think ahead – make the offer from her mother. When the next hostage situation inevitably comes around you can justifiably refer her to your line management.

# Reverse psychology

Telling a child something is the 'forbidden fruit' will only elicit, "Where is it?" Saying things are perfectly OK makes them dull and too easily achievable. Telling them not to do something and then they do it, only for you to tell them not to do it again make them think, "Hey, this guy is not so bright but he is fun". Just tell them to go right ahead. Hah! Knew you couldn't do it 'cos you are a dad! God help us all.

# Techniques to get children to do what you want

Remember this, you live in a house of uncertainty. Mainly for you as a dad. On serious misdemeanour, you may advise total radical circumcision for your eldest boy to the shock of your partner. The very same person who said, "be firm with them, they deserve it". After confronting the entire family she will say, "Come to me my darlings, your father has lost his mind". Next time ask the children what they want and say 'yes' subject to maternal approval.

# How to avoid confrontation

Don't. Leave this to the true conductor of the orchestra. This is the way Kennedy avoided World War over Cuba. Mind you, watch out for the 'grassy knoll'.

# When all else fails....

Children pick up their negotiating skill from their parents and siblings. Simply relying on shouting and doing Basil Fawlty Silly Walks is short term advantage for long term suffering. Listening to what they have to say, giving them time in their own words – not "Are you telling me that…?" – to express themselves, will pay great dividends for the future.

Shouting, "You leave this house now and you don't come back" is a recipe for an empty room not to mention an empty heart.

But then you can always make a few bob out of a lodger.

# Happy MUM SeCtion

The way I see it, the secret to a happy balance at home is based on the following principles... Happy mummy = happy baby = happy daddy with an inane grin.

# Test yourself

## How good a partner are you?

Complete this quiz and find out whether you should be on a promise or in permanent household purgatory.

## 1 The bed

Do you?

a) Make the bed up faithful every day ❏
b) Make up the bed, but forget to add the frilly pillow cases ❏
c) Throw the duvet over a rumpled bed-sheet with a damp spot ❏
d) Throw the duvet over a rumpled bed-sheet with a damp spot on her side ❏

## 2 The loo

Do you?

a) Leave the toilet seat up ❏
b) Replace the toilet paper roll when it is empty ❏
c) Resort to kitchen towel roll when the toilet paper roll is empty ❏
d) Wash your hands in the kitchen sink ❏

## 3 Your body

Do you?

a) Develop a noticeable pot belly ❑

b) Develop a noticeable pot belly
and exercise to get rid of it ❑

c) Say, "It doesn't matter,
you have one too." ❑

## 4 The intruder

Do you?

a) Check out a suspicious noise
and it is nothing ❑

b) Check out a suspicious noise
and it is something ❑

c) Pummel it with a cricket bat ❑

d) Pummel something that turns
out to be her cat ❑

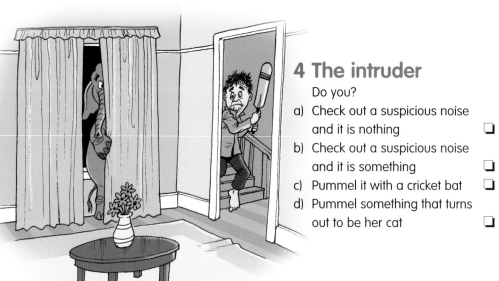

# 5 Her post-natal self-confidence

She asks, "Does this dress make me look fat?"
You reply

a) "Where?" ❑
b) "No, I think it's your bum" ❑
c) "It looked OK on your sister" ❑

# 6 The dress equation

She puts on one dress and shows you another one.
Do you?

a) Choose the dress she isn't wearing ❑
b) Give reasons why you like that dress ❑
c) Say it reminds you of her before the children ❑

# 7 It's her birthday

Do you?

a) Buy her a present ❑
b) Buy her something expensive ❑
c) Buy her a nasal hair trimmer ❑

# 8 She comes home

You don't

a) Notice her new hairstyle ☐
b) Notice her new dress ☐
c) Notice she wearing a gas mask ☐

Add up your scores
1 a) -1, b) 0, c) -1, d) -10
2 a) -5, b) 0, c) -1, d) -100
3 a) -15, b) +10, c) -800
4 a) 0, b) +5, c)+10, d) -40
5 a) -35, b) -100, c) -1000
6 a) -10, b) -20, c) -50
7 a) 0, b) +5, c) -800
8 a) -10, b) -10, c) -800

# If you scored

**10 or more**
You're a great partner and dad you might just see a sparkle in her eye.

**50 or more**
You should think about going into TV. You could help dads all over the world even though your partner is vomiting into your socks.

**100 or more**
You're a fantastic liar. Write a book, like this one.

**Minus 1000 or less**
Welcome to the club Dad.

**Whatever you scored in this brilliantly illuminating quiz we'd like to point out that it's only really a question of the depth of the poo you're in.**

# GROWING UP

'You spend the first two years of their life teaching them to walk and talk. Then you spend the next 16 telling them to sit down and shut up'

Encourage them to play a musical instrument
that doesn't need a JCB to take it to school

## Their music

This is important. Head bopping to Max Monroe as you drive them to school is considered child abuse. Keep the window closed, the volume down and your head firmly fixed in one place. You can do what you want with your legs. Loud music is the prerogative of the young.
A loud bedroom is less likely to damage their hearing as permanently as headphones. Ask why they like music. Try to explain why you prefer pogo to rave. Best of luck, Dad.
This is the chance to talk about them playing a musical instrument themselves. Suggest something which can be transported to school without a JCB.

## TV remote controls

The easiest way to find something lost around the house is to buy a replacement.

"My eldest daughter bought me a wonderful device for Christmas which tracked down the TV remote controller. She then borrowed the device to find her keys. Now I have neither a TV remote controller or device to find it. What I do have is the little sliding cover for the batteries so I press it making bleep-bleep noises."

Buying cable or satellite gives you, a father, greater choice of viewing? Poor deluded fool.

'Mothers of teens now know why some animals eat their young'

# Room boom (untidy rooms)

Once you get used to finding plates of food sporting a growth Alexander Fleming would be proud of, the pairs of yellow underpants which started life the colour white come as light relief.

Never, ever put a naked hand under your teenage son's bed. Use a shovel. It will be quicker and you can sterilise a shovel.

The world over, teenage daughters tights are still being investigated by Hans Blix. Families fall out over untidy rooms. In truth your children will soon be leaving the family home and the room once threatened with bricking up becomes a shrine. Yes, I know. Total crap. Use a flamethrower on it.

**Never, ever put a naked hand under your teenage son's bed**

39

# EATING

## Foodie
(Vegetarian vs Carnivore)

## Natural Foods
It is worth reminding your potential veggie offspring set to eat a lot of natural foods that most people die of natural causes.

Dismissing eating habits as a fad they 'grow out of' will serve only to undermine your relationship as most young people become vegetarians out of principle not fetish. Now is the chance to encourage them to cook for themselves. On the plus side, a carrot is generally cheaper than a sirloin although prepared foods can be prohibitively expensive and have questionable health benefits.

## Eating out
Taking children to eat out in public is fraught with pitfalls as they push for fast food and dangerous levels of sugar and you want to eat where grown-ups are known to frequent. There are some hard and fast rules though.

If colouring weren't added to cola, it would be green – not unlike teeth afterwards.

Fast food is so called because the average adult would rather fast  than eat it.
Children on the other hand, universally adore it. Not least because of the informality.
Go for 'regular' (it used to be called 'small' in English) unless you want your kids to look like the Michelin Man. 'Super large' is a prediction of girth not a food portion.

'Real' food is undoubtedly harder to find on a main street these days, but worth looking for. With it comes table manners and basic things like knives and forks rather than just napkins for fingers. Also, chips actually look as though they started life as a potato.

# CINEMA

Just in case you haven't been to the silver screen for a while, there are no 'B films any more. Forget two films for your money. They are all B films.

## Buy your tickets by web

Booking by phone takes even longer than the film itself but is a great way of learning numbers from 1 to 10. Pressing the wrong numbers on the telephone keypad can get you and your young children into multiplex seats carrying a health warning to those with a pathological fear of chainsaws.

## Bring healthy food with you

Cnemas are determined to create more child extras for The Blob with sugar-rich cola served in disposable fire-buckets. Know you will be the only one crying as they will have seen the pirate copy five times before you took them on their treat to the cinema.

## Realise there is no intermission

There is no ice-cream lady. There is no newsreel. There is no 'B' film. What do you want for €50?

# SLEEPING OVER

'The main purpose of holding children's parties is to remind yourself that there are children more awful than your own'

Sleepovers may involve checking out other parents

In effect this means you have to drive them to the temporary home, check the resident parent or parents have no criminal records, their fridge has less than four weeks growth on the yoghurt and none of the siblings appeared in The House on 49th Street.

By way of return you must allow the child's mother to inspect your basement/ loft/ chainsaw.

On the plus side, no bedside stories for the duration of the sleepover.

# MONEY ISSUES...

ie, the things that are going to cost you your golf club membership!

## Pocket money

Most children interpret this as 'money you take out of Dad's pocket'. Pocket money only covers the most basic luxuries for a child. Expect to pay for everything and write their pocket money off as a tip. It is not tax-deductible.

By all means try to link pocket money to household chores like washing the car or cleaning their rooms. This is the advice given by child experts, the criteria for working in this field is not to have any children of their own.

Most adolescents see performance-related pay as an infringement of their basic human right to remain horizontal until at least 1pm on a weekend.

## Telephones

Brace yourself. Those buff-white envelopes from the telephone company will never be the same again, especially if you have teenage daughters.

For some reason only known to owners of two X chromosomes, teenage daughters attract telephone bills like ships collect barnacles. Unfortunately, unlike barnacles, you can't get rid of the account demands.

Putting an egg timer next to the phone and demanding they check it afterwards often only results in hard-boiled attitudes.

'Children seldom misquote you. In fact, they usually repeat word for word what you shouldn't have said'

## Clothes and style
All kids want to be cool and the same as their friends.

# RULES FOR DADS

- - - - - - - - - - - - - - - - - - - - - - - - - - - - - - - - - - - -

Walk at least four paces behind your teenage daughter at all times.

- - - - - - - - - - - - - - - - - - - - - - - - - - - - - - - - - - - -

Never attempt to link arms unless you are wearing at least
one designer article and under no circumstance if sporting
your favourite pair of sandals.

- - - - - - - - - - - - - - - - - - - - - - - - - - - - - - - - - - - -

No matter how outlandish she looks, swoon you fool.

- - - - - - - - - - - - - - - - - - - - - - - - - - - - - - - - - - - -

Asking your teenage daughter why she is wearing
a pair of underpants on her head is not funny.
"YOU ARE NOT MY FATHER" is a standard response
and one you may sympathise with at the time.

- - - - - - - - - - - - - - - - - - - - - - - - - - - - - - - - - - - -

Always get the last word in. Apologise for style crimes with
a large donation to her taxi fare or party dress fund.

- - - - - - - - - - - - - - - - - - - - - - - - - - - - - - - - - - - -

A long hug from your daughter is worth it even if you recognise
the smell from her trendy head-gear.

- - - - - - - - - - - - - - - - - - - - - - - - - - - - - - - - - - - -

Never interfere with their choice of clothes or offer advice
no matter how ridiculous they look.
Remember, it makes for great material at their 21st/wedding.

- - - - - - - - - - - - - - - - - - - - - - - - - - - - - - - - - - - -

Boys on the other hand don't wear clothes.
They merely tolerate your choice with a smile
not unlike the Joker in Batman.

- - - - - - - - - - - - - - - - - - - - - - - - - - - - - - - - - - - -

# THINGS YOU NEED TO TALK ABOUT

## Outing of Santa Claus

Never underestimate the strength of belief in Santa Claus. While God might be pretty nifty at dividing the Red Sea, only Santa Claus can leave a bag-full of presents on their legs on 25th December.

## School reports

Grades are of no consequence. Nor are the comments that 'John could do better if only he would apply himself less to computer sites promising free downloads on perfectly harmless examples of adult behaviour' (credit card required).

## The best ways to act:

- Let them see you reading their report and smiling
- Compliment your child on their achievements however small they may seem to you.
- Don't compare them with other children, especially their brothers or sisters.
- Avoid recalling how well you did at school/how much it has cost you to send them to school etc.
- Pick something out and comment positively about it even if it is something off the mainstream.
- Boosting their confidence from their report will always produce better results than hitting them over the head with it.
- Take their report into a small quiet room and cry, manfully.

## Sex

Under-confidence is universal. Never underestimate a teenage boy's lack of insight into sex, his body and control over it. Now is the time to talk openly about it. There is a lack of information on sex for boys so they get most information from their friends or, increasingly, the web. Given the nature of many of web sites don't be surprised if they end up thinking a chainsaw is required for normal sex.

Girls, on the other hand, get loads of info from teenage girls' magazines, but there is no male equivalent.

What you think they need to know is not always what they want to know.

Be prepared to answer questions that would make your granny's toes curl.

We take teaching them about road safety and wearing seat belts for granted, yet baulk when addressing sex. Not using a condom can be a whole lot more dangerous than not using a seat belt.

'We childproofed our homes, but they are still getting in'

## Sexuality

Much as it might hurt some Dads, sexuality is in truth a broad spectrum. Your son or daughter confiding in you that they might not see sexuality just quite the same way as Mum and Dad may be a terrible shock, but also a tribute to their confidence in you as a parent. This is the big test. Are they any less your son or daughter? Your response will let them know in no uncertain terms.

## Computer downloads

Give a child a fish and they feed them for a day; teach them to use the Internet and they won't bother you for weeks.

The average computer user blinks 7 times a minute. Obsessives blink at the same rate as the cursor. Talking to a computer freak can make susceptible people have a seizure.

There are packages which limit viewing and even sites. In truth most children are capable of disabling them as quickly as you can think of an excuse for watching 'late nite TV'.

Talking about it is more productive

**You may be surprised at what they know**

# FIRST AID

Most accidental injuries are minor and can be treated using simple first aid measures but in the unlikely event of a serious accident or sudden illness, knowledge of first aid techniques could help you to save your child's life. You should get professional training rather than waiting for it to happen first.

By following the basic guidelines provided here you will be able to deal with most day-to-day accidents and injuries. Information on dealing with emergencies is also provided.

The key things to remember in any emergency situation are:

- Remain calm and confident
- Do all you can to help
  but don't put yourself in danger
- Do not give the person anything to eat or drink

# Is my baby really ill?

Parents are usually good at noticing when something is not quite right with their baby but it can be difficult to know what is wrong.

**HERE ARE SOME SIGNS THAT CAN BE IMPORTANT, IF THE BABY:**
- Is not responding to you normally.
- Is unusually drowsy or not interested in looking at you, even when awake.
- Is not interested in feeding.
- Feels floppy or limp when cuddled or lifted.
- Has a cry that seems different (perhaps moaning, whimpering or shrill), and soothing doesn't help.

# Other signs of illness

If you are already worried and then notice other problems too (like those in the list below), call the doctor for advice.

**IF THE BABY:**
- Looks very pale.
- Is irritable and does not like being touched.
- Has a new rash.
- Has bruised or discoloured skin.
- Is hot (feverish or has a temperature).
- Is breathless or is breathing much faster than usual.
- Starts being sick (vomiting).

# When taking a young child to hospital

**Reassure them and explain that you're going together to see the doctor at the hospital to make things better.**

**Take a favourite toy with you.**

**Dress your child in a coat or a dressing gown over their nightclothes, or dress your child fully.**
It doesn't matter which one, do what seems most sensible.

**Arrange care for other children.**
If this is not possible, take them as well (it is not wise to leave a child at home without an adult there to look after them).

**Don't forget to leave a note.**
And take your keys and wallet with you as well as your mobile phone if you have one.

# Bites and stings

Insect bites and stings can be painful but they are not usually serious, even in children. Most can be treated with simple, common-sense remedies without needing the attention of your doctor.

- Apply a cold compress, such as a bag of frozen peas in a tea-towel, to insect bites and stings.
- Remove bee stings with tweezers by gripping the base of the sting nearest to the skin to avoid squeezing the poison sac.
- Remove ticks by covering them with a smear of petroleum jelly/ Vaseline, which blocks their breathing holes, and causes them to drop off.
- Simply pulling at the tick or trying to burn it off can leave the head in the skin, leading to infection.

**SEEK MEDICAL ATTENTION IF:**
- The child has a known allergy to bites and stings.
- The sting cannot be removed.
- There is infection around the site.
- There is a fever or shortness of breath.
- Animal bites need urgent medical attention, as they may become infected if not treated.
  Small animal bites should be thoroughly cleaned with soap and water and covered with a sterile dressing. For serious bites, apply direct pressure with a clean cloth (as described above) to control the bleeding.

# Burns and scalds

Any burn or scald requires immediate action.
- Remove any tight clothing if possible.
- Cool the affected area with cold water for at least 10 minutes, then cover with a light, non-fluffy material. For a limb, kitchen film or a polythene bag may be used.
- Don't burst any blisters and don't apply any cream or ointments.
- The exception is mild sunburn which may be soothed with a lotion like calamine.

**SEEK MEDICAL ATTENTION IF:**
- The burn is larger than half the size of the child's hand.
- The burn is on the face.
- The skin is broken.

**SEVERE BURNS NEED URGENT MEDICAL ATTENTION**
Cool the burn down, cover it with a sterile dressing, and take the child to your local accident and emergency department immediately or call for an ambulance. While waiting for the ambulance, lay them down and raise their legs. This helps keep blood available for the vital organs. Don't remove clothes if they are sticking to the skin.

# Cuts and grazes

For a minor cut, press the wound with a clean fabric pad for a few minutes to help stop the bleeding.
For a cut on an arm or leg, elevate the limb.
Water may be used to wipe around the edge of the cut or graze.
Once clean, apply a sterile dressing, e.g. a plaster.

**SEEK MEDICAL ATTENTION IF:**
- **The cut is deep cut and the edges cannot be pulled together.** Severe redness or swelling develops after a couple of days (this may be a sign of an infection).
- **Severe bleeding from a wound needs immediate medical attention.** While waiting for expert help, lay the child down and raise the injured part of the body above the level of the heart to help reduce blood loss. Place a clean cloth against the wound and press firmly. Secure this pad in place. **Never use a tourniquet.**

# Nose bleeds

Nose bleeds are common and most are easily dealt with.
- Sit the child down, leaning slightly forward, and tell them to breathe through their mouth.
- Then pinch the nose firmly for about 10 minutes.
- Seek medical help if the bleeding continues for more than 30 minutes or if you suspect the nose is broken.

# Sprains, strains and bruising

Remember 'RICE' (rest, ice, compress, elevation).
Rest the injured part of the body as much as possible. Immediately after the injury, pack the area with ice wrapped in a cloth - a bag of frozen peas works well - to reduce swelling. Keep the ice in place for about 10 minutes. Gently compress the injury and bind the area with an elastic bandage so it is well supported, but make sure it doesn't restrict blood flow. To minimise swelling, keep the injured part elevated as much of the time as possible.

**SEEK MEDICAL ATTENTION IF:**
- **You think there may be a broken bone.**
  Immobilise the area with padding and seek aid immediately.
- **Symptoms don't improve.**
- **Bruising remains after several days.**

# Head injuries

Bangs on the head are common, particularly amongst children. Few need the attention of your doctor, but occasionally a head injury can cause bleeding inside the skull, which needs urgent attention. This bleeding can take place soon after the injury, or up to 6 months later. For a minor knock or bump to the head, sit the child down as they may be dizzy, and place a cold, damp cloth on the affected area. You may want to provide a basin in case they vomit.

**SEEK URGENT MEDICAL ATTENTION IF:**
- **They talk about double vision or can't hear you.**
- **Repeated vomiting, fits or convulsions occur.**
- **They are confused.**
- **Discharge appears from the nose, eyes or ears.**
- **The pain continues after three days.**
- **Remember that these symptoms appear some time after the initial incident.**
  If they do, visit your doctor.

# Poisoning

Accidental poisoning is one of the most common reasons for children to need emergency treatment. If you suspect your child may have eaten or drunk something dangerous seek expert medical advice immediately. You can provide important help for the doctors by trying to find out what has caused the poisoning, how much was taken and when, and by taking any containers and remains of tablets, liquids, plants or samples of vomit to the hospital with you.

If the child becomes unconscious, place them in the recovery position and if breathing stops, begin mouth-to-mouth resuscitation following the procedure described at the beginning of this section.

**NEVER TRY TO INDUCE VOMITING BY ANY MEANS!**

# Choking

Choking happens surprisingly often. Immediate action is vital, so it is important to know the correct steps to follow:

- **Check inside the mouth, and remove any obstruction**
If you can't see or feel any obstruction, bend the child over your hand or lap and give them 5 taps (not hard slaps) between their shoulder blades.

- **If there is no response, turn them over and using two fingers**
Only press firmly in their breast bone five times.

- **Glass of water?**
If the blockage is not completely cleared, or the child continues to have trouble breathing, start again while someone seeks urgent medical attention.

# EMERGENCIES

## Seek URGENT medical attention for:

- Head injury with bleeding from eyes, ears or nose, drowsiness or vomiting.
- Loss of consciousness.
- Broken bone or dislocation.
- Severe chest pain or breathlessness.
- Sudden severe abdominal pain that won't go away.
- Unresolved choking and difficulty breathing.
- Severe bleeding.

# How to deal with an emergency

## Getting help

Sometimes, the quickest way of getting medical help is to take the child directly to the accident and emergency department of your local hospital.

**But call an ambulance and do not move the child if:**
- You think they have a back or neck injury, or any other injury that could be made worse by movement.
- The child is unconscious or has stopped breathing, and needs your constant attention.

# The recovery position

This is a safe position for an unconscious child, which allows easy breathing and prevents choking if they vomit. After checking they are breathing normally, turn them on their side. Ensure that the airway is clear with the jaw pulled forward and their head tipped slightly back.

# Mouth-to-mouth resuscitation

**Note: You can damage a baby's lungs by blowing into their mouth.** Better to do so by letting your chest naturally fall without forcing the breath out. Or blow through a cupped hand over nose and mouth together – this dilutes the power of your breath. Check first for anything obstructing the airway inside the mouth.

# Cardio-pulmonary resuscitation (CPR)

Check for a pulse (use their upper arm on the inside).

1 **If there is no breathing or pulse start CPR.**
   Remember it is different for babies and small children.
2 **Place the baby in the same position as for mouth-to-mouth resuscitation.**
3 **Imagine a line between the baby's nipples.**
   Place your finger tips of two fingers just below the mid point of this line.
4 **Press at the rate of 100 per minute**
   **moving the chest down no more than 2cm with each press.**
5 **Give 5 compressions to each single mouth-to-mouth breath.**
   For small children use one hand only at about 100 compressions per minute moving the chest downwards no more than 3cm.

# Telephone 999 for an ambulance.

Keep other important numbers readily available by noting them on the pages at the front of this guide, or program them into your mobile phone.

# Emergencies and babies

## 1 Lay the baby on a firm surface
Tilt back the head and lift the chin to open the air passages.

## 2 Check to see if they are breathing for 10 seconds
One way is to put a mirror to their mouth to see if it steams up.
If they are place them in the recovery position described above.

## 3 Cover the mouth and nose with your mouth and give a gentle breath
Their chest should rise.

## 4 Allow their chest to fall and give 5 more breaths
at about 20 per minute

## 5 Check whether they are breathing on their own
If not continue

## Shock (loss of blood)

Children in shock may become pale, sweaty, drowsy and confused. They need urgent medical attention. Phone 999. While waiting for help, remain calm but do not give them anything to eat or drink. If they are unconscious lay them on their back with their legs raised, loosen any tight clothing and keep them warm.

## Broken bones and dislocation

Broken bones and dislocations always need immediate medical attention. They can be very painful, and you can help by reassuring the child and keeping them still.

## Broken limbs

Steady and support the limb with your hands. If a leg is broken, place padding around it to prevent movement. A broken arm or collar bone should be supported on the affected side of the body.

## Injured neck or spine

Keep the injured child as still as possible without heavily restraining them. It is essential not to move someone with a neck or spine injury unless they are in imminent danger of further injury. If the casualty becomes unconscious, carefully place them in recovery position while keeping the spine in line at all times.

## Dislocated joints

Never try to force a joint back into place. Simply support the limb and seek emergency help.

# FATHER'S DAY

Mothers will be the first to point out that Father's Day is an American invention designed more to generate income for card manufacturers than restore inequality when it comes to breakfast in bed.

Soap-on a-rope, socks, 'Daft Dad Mugs' and CDs of music from groups you assumed were weapons of mass destruction are par for the course.
You must welcome them as readily as you devour their proffered breakfast tray of egg 'a la' whale oil avec porcine outer side.
Smile dad. Eat up the toast.
Carbon is good for the digestion.

# Be nice to your kids. They will choose your nursing home one day.

**Register at www.dadssurvival.com** for more information delivered to your desktop.

# IAN BANKS

In a previous life Ian Banks was once a television repair man. He might not be able to cure you but he can do wonders for your vertical hold. He has four children, delivering one himself. "Not quite the same as child birth but at least I got to shout 'push'".

While working part-time as a family doctor and A&E officer in Belfast, he also represents GPs for the British Medical Association and is a member of Council for the UK. Being a trustee for the Doctor Patient Partnership and chairman of Advancing Self Care (ASC) fits with his role as the official spokesman on men's health issues for the BMA, president of the European Mens Health Forum and the England & Wales Men's Health Forum and for six years the medical editor for The Men's Health Magazine.

The BBC book 'The Trouble with Men' was written by Ian in 1996 to accompany the television series of the same name. It was followed by Men's Health, The Good Patient Guide, The Children's Health Guide, Get Fit with Brittas, Men's Health in General Practice, Ask About Sex and the 50th NHS Anniversary book from the NHSE/HEA The Home Medicine Guide. He is also the author of the NHS Direct Healthcare Guide and Web site.".

Ian is the editor of the Men's Health Journal and the UEMO Clinical Journal. His latest books are "The Ultimate Dad's Survival Guide", the Haynes "Man Workshop Manual" the Haynes "Baby Workshop Manual" and the Haynes Sex Workshop Manual. He is currently working on the Haynes "Woman Workshop Manual" and the Haynes "Cancer Manual". Home is a small GM free farm in Northern Ireland.